MARKET STRUCTURE AND LIQIDITY TRADING USING INSTITUTIONAL CANDLE, FLIP ZONE AND IMBALANCE

BY Austin Walker

Standard Market Structure

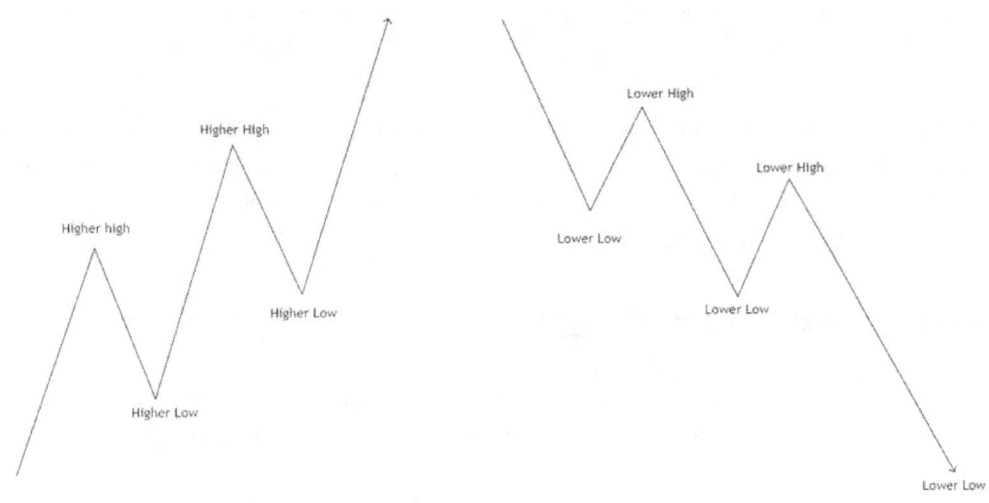

Key thing to know, when we're looking at TradingView data, broker data, from one brokerage to another, or one data feed that you're using on TradingView (for instance Oanda vs FXCM), you'll notice that wicks will differ. And why does that happen? Each broker has access to different liquidity pools and fills, therefore price data feed they offer will slightly vary from broker to broker. So essentially, when you are trading with a brokerage, your spreads tend to increase or decrease depending on volatility in market conditions and you can usually see that on a chart in the form of wicks. But if you're comparing the overall price action between one data provider and another, the one thing that generally speaking remains very true are the candle bodies. You'll see a little bit of difference when you're mapping out wicks when you're looking at one broker, one wick maybe in the denoted place, but on another broker, it might be actually above.

Market structure shows us as institutional trader where the large majority of buy and sell positions are being placed in the market; it illustrates what positions the banks are currently in (net long/short) and the next major trade they could be placing. Market structure is the first 'brick layer' of the house. Without understanding these concepts there is no foundation to your trading. When you are able to understand structure from a macro (Monthly, weekly) and micro (5,3,1 minute TF) perspective, that will put you at the top 1% of your game, as you will understand when the banks are going to take their next impulsive move in their specific bias. Then once you have your AOI (area of interest), we can react accordingly on the micro timeframe to get a pin point sniper entry and hold for long last RR trades.

This will often be used on the bigger Timeframes: Monthly, Weekly, Daily and sometimes 4 Hour. It gives us on overview in what direction price is going to trade impulsively. If we are making HH's and HL's on the daily timeframe, we should expect a new bullish trend continuation until we reach a valid AOI.

Multiplex Market Structure (Bullish)

There are two different Market structure types we look at: internal and external structure. When we have internal structure, we have something called a multiplex structure.

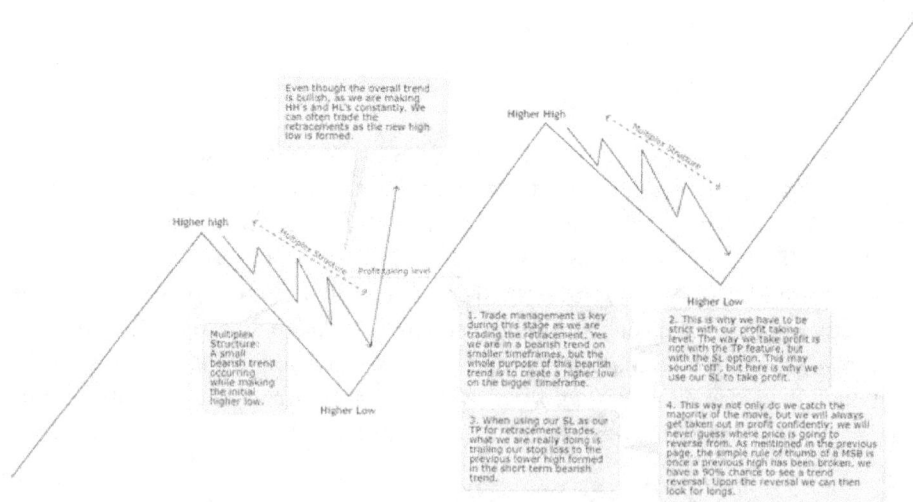

The best thing when trading a multiplex structure, that's internal structure, is to always start on the higher timeframes to get a general understanding of how price is moving. Are we moving upwards creating higher highs and higher lows or are we moving downwards creating lower highs and lower lows? Once you've determined that it becomes more straight forward dropping down timeframes to determine the market structure on those timeframes and correlating them. When specific bias is understood, we can counter trade that specific trend if structure is present on the smaller/micro timeframes. The diagram above is an accurate representation on how we would go about trading a multiplex structure.

Multiplex Market Structure (Bearish)

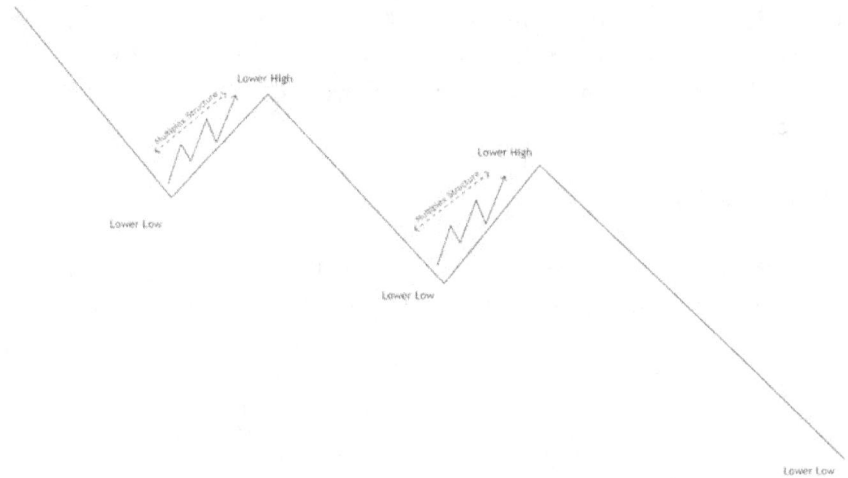

The HTF will always be our main interest but because the markets are fractal, you'll be able to utilize LTF just as strongly. This meaning, we can use the multiplex structure to counter trend the main bias; this will also allow us to hedge our position meaning we have capitalized on both sides of the market.

Multiplex Structure + hedging

When we take our multiplex structural trades, these are normally done in a counter trend environment which is not the best scenario, however we can make the multiplex structure a lot more counter intuitive by taking multiplex trades at HTF AOI.

Break of Market Structure (3 different types)

By understanding structure, we will have multiple opportunities to get into the market but how we become great traders is by minimizing our losses i.e. we take less losses as our losses are capped at 1%. We want to only get into the sponsor candles that have the highest probability of working out - where price will tap and react off instantly.

This is really important for us. If we don't know what sponsor candle to put entry on especially on the lower timeframes - we can get into a lot of bad positions. A lot of things can look like sponsor candles on the LTF, but they are actually already mitigated. We want to have maximum precision and look for real valid "not yet tested sponsor candles" after BMS, because this will avoid us to go further on already filled orders. By waiting for a clear BMS illustrates that big banks and funds are in that move and gives us a good confluence to take the move.

1. Minor BMS (mBMS)

This occurs on the smaller timeframes; normally on 15m timeframe and below. We will see an initial move in the specific direction banks look to buy/sell the currency pair on the smaller timeframe first.

2. Significant break of the market structure (SBOS)

This occurs on the 15m - 1HR timeframe. This indicates a major amount of buy/sell orders are coming into the market. When we witness a significant break in market structure with an impulsive move bullishly/bearishly, we can then decide to go long/short upon a mitigation. This is because the reasoning of that significant market structure break big banks have brought into that move. Here is an example below.

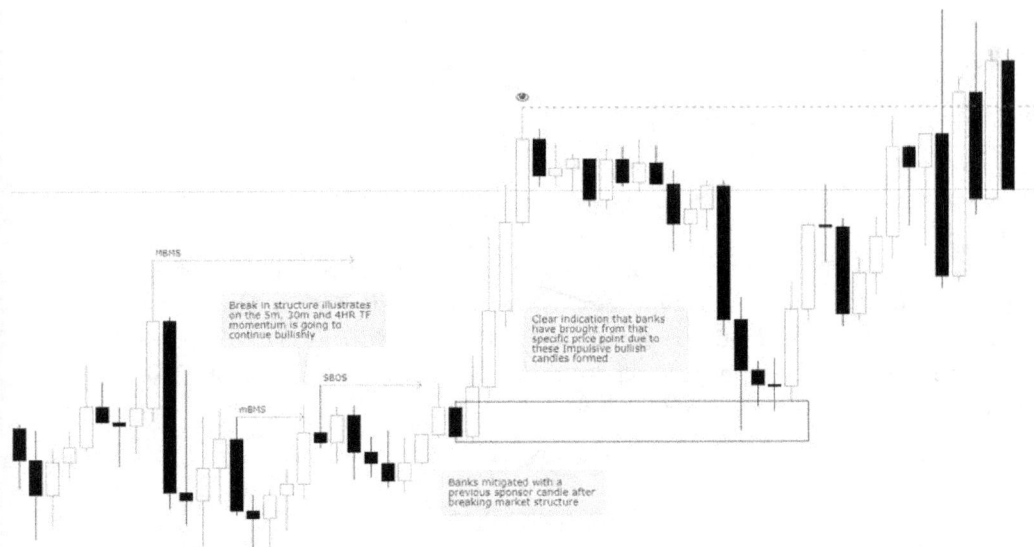

Break in structure illustrates
on the 5m, 30m and 4HR TF
momentum is going to
continue bullishly

Clear indication that banks
have brought from that
specific price point due to
these impulsive bullish
candles formed

MBMS

SBOS

mBMS

Banks mitigated with a
previous sponsor candle after
breaking market structure

3. Major Market Structure

This is formed on the Daily Timeframe and above. By us scaling into these larger timeframes we can identify where the majority of smart money positions are placed. If we are constantly breaking market structure bullishly on the weekly timeframe and making HH's/HL's we understand the majority of smart money are long, then we can refine our AOI on smaller timeframes (AOI will be discussed on a smaller timeframe).

Example, if we are looking at an overall daily uptrend, so we're putting in higher highs and higher lows and we start to see on the 4 Hour and 1 Hour that price is making lower lows and lower highs, we might immediately be thinking that we are in a downtrend and that we should only be looking for sells. Well, that may be true on an intraday perspective. One thing we have to keep in mind is what is the higher time frame suggesting from a structural standpoint.

If we know that we are in a heavy bull trend and the price is more than likely going to move to the upside, the lower lows that we're seeing on those time frame charts are more than likely a pullback or retracement phase of that daily chart. So when we have that information in mind we can frame our trades in a completely different manner and especially when we take that one step further and we're looking at 15 minute, 5 minute and 1 minute charts, it is so easy to get lost in those market structures when things are constantly switching from bull to bear, bear to bull and vice a versa.

That's when it ultimately comes down to looking at the higher time frame charts and remaining grounded on the actual momentum and the overall trade idea that you're trading. I hope this gives a little bit of insight of the various approaches of mapping market structure as well as identifying breaks of market structure.

Momentum in the Break of Market Structure

There are two main things we look for:
1. A large body candle that forms imbalance
2. A continuation of these candles

We want to see a committed push breaking structure not an immediate retrace back. If price breaks structure and immediately retraces then this signals weak order flow in that direction. We're trying to identify where large orders are being placed in the markets. If price immediately retraces after breaking structure that tells us there isn't a lot of power behind that move so it likely won't be sustained.

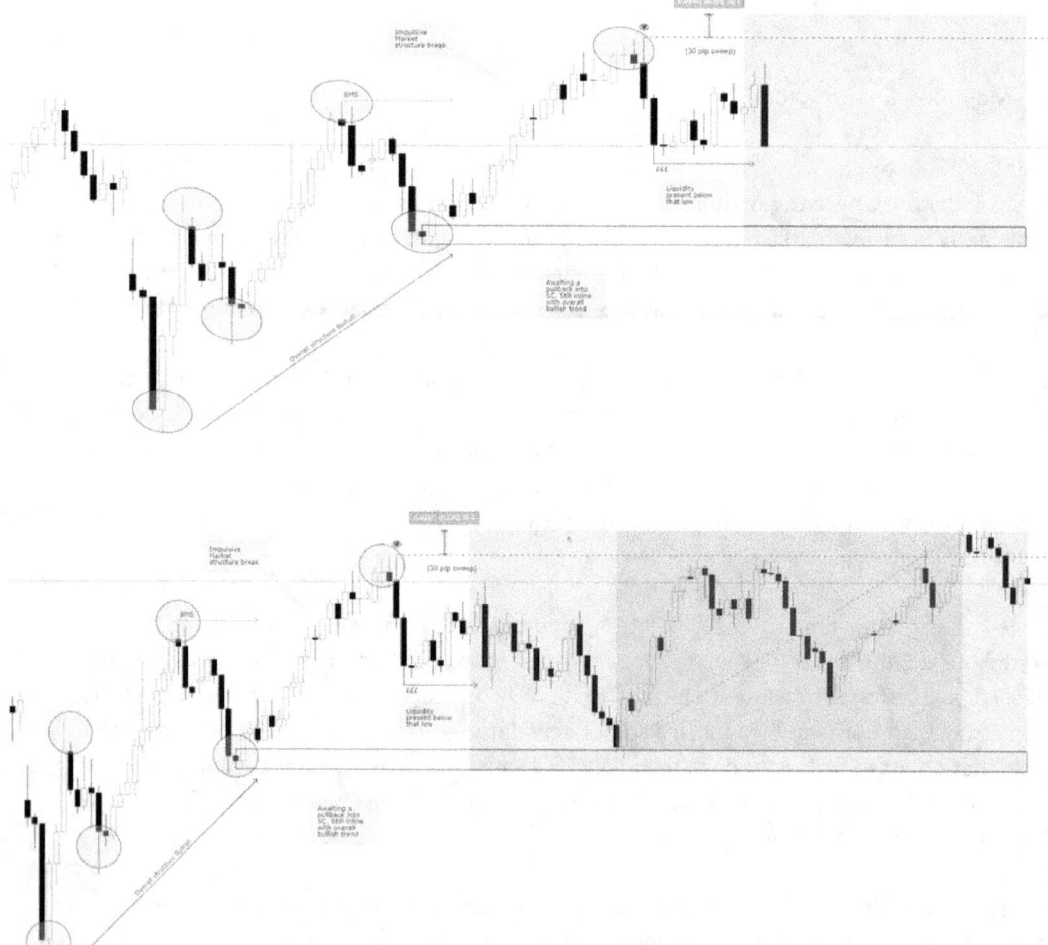

MARKET STRUCTURE 2

What should form the foundation of your trading knowledge? What is the most important thing to learn in the beginning? Is it fundamental or technical analysis? Should you master candlestick/chart patterns or Moving Averages first?

What is the backbone of any financial market?

It is PRICE.

Therefore learning how to read PRICE should be your starting point. Mastering reading price will lay foundation of your trading career. Building everything else will come after that.

There are 3 steps a trader goes through when learning about price:
- o   what we think price looks like
- o   what we believe the reality of price looks like
- o the hard reality

Reading a trend is easy, right?

If I draw a line from point A to point B like this...

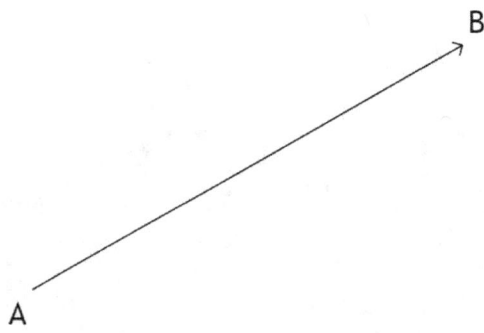

...is it uptrend or downtrend?

And if I draw a line from point A to point B like this...

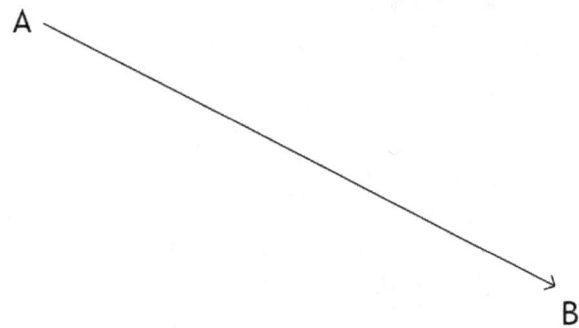

...is it bullish or bearish? It is easy to answer, right?

This is what we think price looks like.

But have you ever seen price move from one point to another in straight line? Is this how the bullish or bearish trend looks like?

Of course, not.

Let's take a look now at what we believe price movement looks like.

What type of trend are we in?

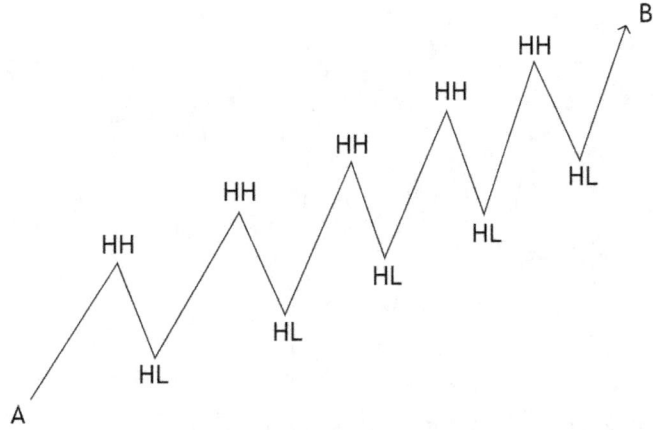

How about now? Is it downtrend or uptrend?

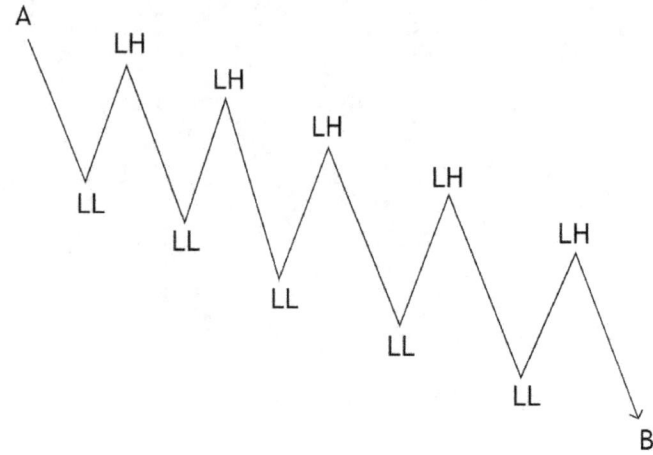

Now this is closer to the reality of how we believe the price on the chart looks like.

But how often can we see price look like that?

NEVER.

In reality price looks more like this.

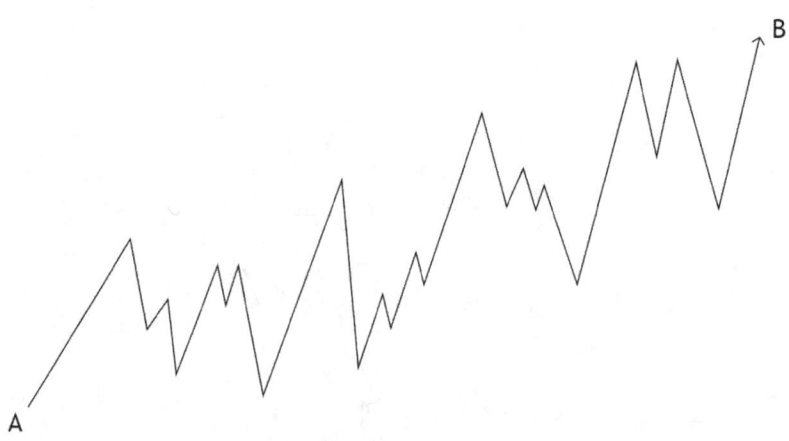

This is another example what you could see on the chart.

MARKET STRUCTURE 2

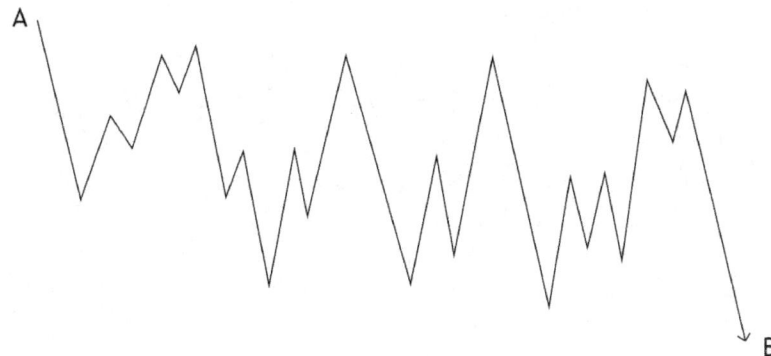

This is more realistic. This is hard reality of how you will see price on the chart. When you see price move like that, it is harder to recognize whether you are in an uptrend or in a downtrend.

In order to remove guesswork from price analysis, we need to introduce rules. This will help us to avoid subjectivity and confusion.

The road to consistency in trading leads through rule-based trading.

If you consistently look at the price chart the same way, do the analysis the same way, look for the same type of patterns/trading opportunities and you consistently execute them, you should be able to achieve consistent results.

Let's review the rules using drawings.

ISP = Initial Structural Point
ISH = Initial Structural High
BMS = Break of Market Structure

MARKET STRUCTURE 2

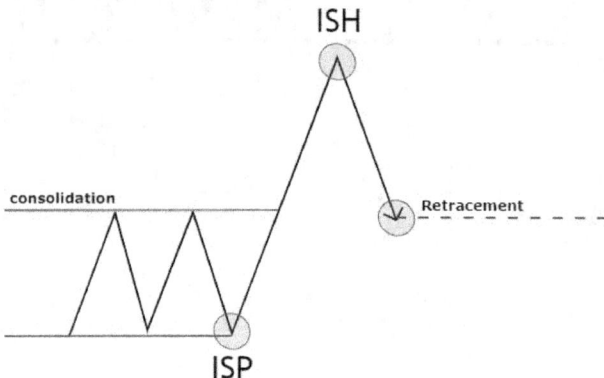

Price has moved out of consolidation, established Initial Structural High and made retracement.

Is this a trend? No, it isn't.

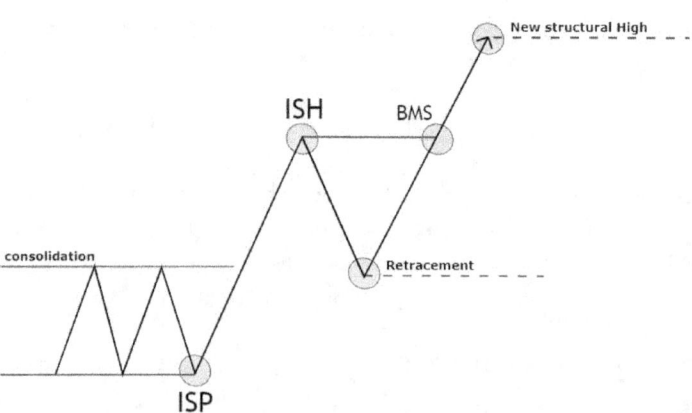

Here we can see how after the initial retracement the ISH has been broken and New Structural High has been established.

Is this a trend? Yes, it is.

MARKET STRUCTURE 2

You can see now, there is no guesswork anymore.

For new trend to be in place, there are 2 main elements we need to identify:
1. new structural high
2. retracement before last new structural high

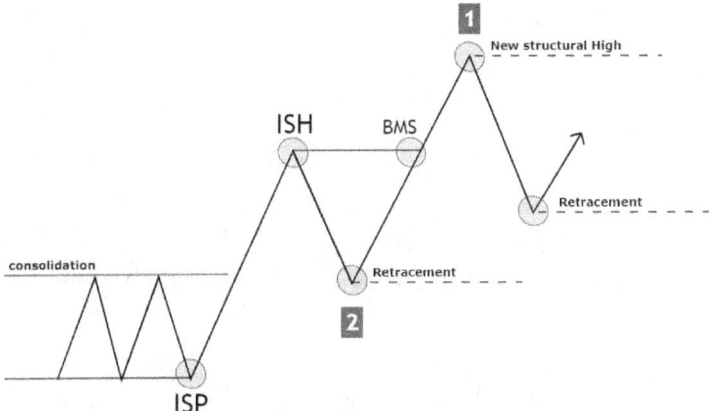

These 2 main elements are going to be our Decision Points. Based on which point is broken first, we will either confirm the trend or invalidate it.

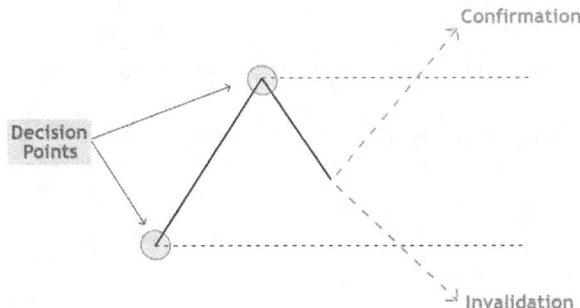

Now you can apply the rules and on the image below you can see we are in bullish trend.

MARKET STRUCTURE 2

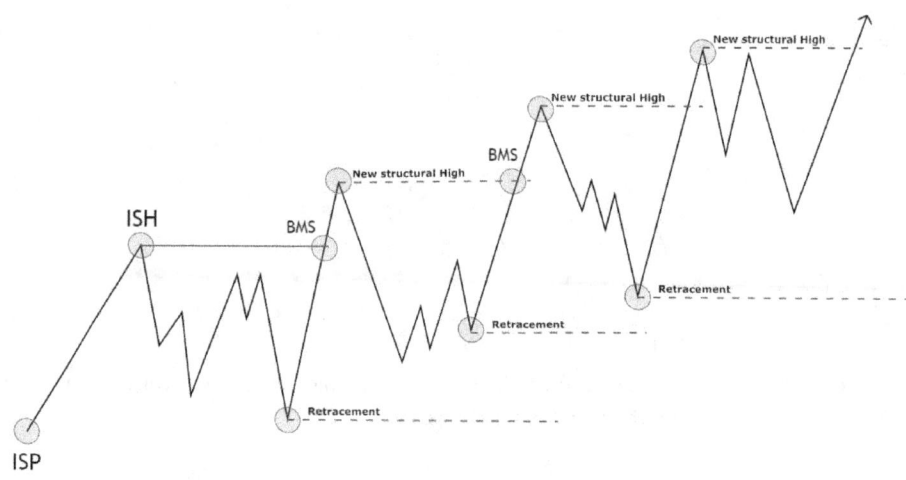

It is very important that you set rules for confirmation and invalidation of the trend.

Now that you have rules, you should be more confident at determining trend direction.

<u>LIQUIDITY</u>

<u>Where is liquidity found in the market</u>

1. Retail traders place sell stops under lows and buy stops above highs, this is where our focus should be, however we should be monitoring this area, not trading off it. We await to see a reaction. The reaction we wait for is those equal highs/lows to be taken out; this is because retail traders see equal highs/equal lows as support and resistance, hence why they put pending orders at this area, or take a trade early at support and resistance due to retail traders seeing a previous reaction off that area and then selling from there. This then builds liquidity in the market for banks to use to move price lower. The longer a "support or resistance" has been holding for, the more liquidity will be valid in that area, which leads to a impulsive move created by banks.

LIQUIDITY

Liquidity pool

2. Liquidity pool is an establishment level in the market where stops and orders would be resting, leaving these areas exposed for smart money to hunt these areas taking stop losses and triggering new buy/sell orders that may be present in that area. Buy stops and sell stops are sources of liquidity above and below short term and long term highs and lows. Liquidity can also be engineered, meaning the banks AI create a equal short term high/low, for them to generate liquidity, then take out that liquidity to use to send price in the opposite direction.

Buy and sell side liquidity

3. Buy and sell side liquidity are areas of price in which buy stops or sell stops are mostly residing. When we understand the higher timeframe, we can see where 'smart money' are possibly going to go long and short due to areas of price creating "support and resistance". Price will use these areas to seek liquidity in order to reverse or continue within its expansion move.

LIQUIDITY

When price is making a double top at a resistance, retail traders see this as a sign to short, which in most cases, however, a majority of the retail traders enter the market too early. Price takes out the Equal Highs triggering the stop losses on early sellers and most importantly triggers the buy stops to pickup liquidity, then moves in the intended direction. Similar applies in the opposite scenario with double bottoms.

Now think about it, how many times have you been trapped or took a loss from a setup similar to these scenarios? It happens to retail traders over and over again because they do not understand the reasoning behind the setups. Most retail traders are taught to buy a double bottom and to sell double top. Now that you understand these patterns and how market makers use them, you will be able to see these manipulated moves occur and then enter the market after the manipulation is complete and you have confirmations to enter the market.

An example is illustrated below:

LIQUIDITY DIAGRAM

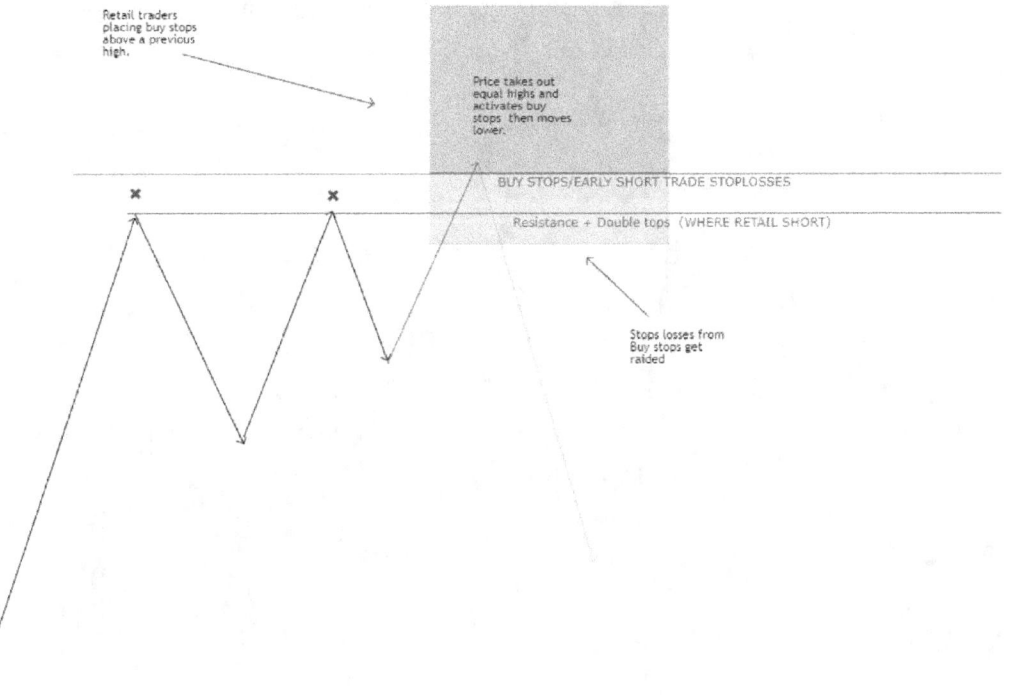

Retail traders placing buy stops above a previous high.

Price takes out equal highs and activates buy stops then moves lower.

BUY STOPS/EARLY SHORT TRADE STOPLOSSES

Resistance + Double tops (WHERE RETAIL SHORT)

Stops losses from Buy stops get raided

LIQUIDITY LIVE EXAMPLE

Examples of Liquidity Pools

Swing high/low
Equal highs/lows (EQH, EQL)
Session (Asian, London, NY) high/low
Daily/Weekly/Monthly high/low

SPONSOR CANDLE

What is a Sponsor Candle

Sponsor candle is a set of orders to buy or sell, as appropriate, set by an institutional price to make the reverse and drives hard in the direction of the trend. The Sponsor candle is a specific price level, is a specific candle.

The usefulness of this concept is to provide high-precision inputs. A Sponsor candle provides you with information on where there is a high probability of price reversal. It's a technique for taking pullbacks in trend with high precision input, allowing inputs of low risk and high benefit ratio.

There are two types of SC, Bullish and Bearish SC. A Bullish SC is specifically a red bearish candle preceding the upward movement. The bullish SC is the last bearish candle before the bullish movement, that breaks market structure higher. This illustrating a high possibility of holding price when price returns to it.

A Bearish SC is highlighted in the same way, but instead of a down move preceding an up move, a bearish SC is created by an up move before a down move, which resumes the downtrend, makes new lows and/or breaks market structure. These levels are created by institutional short sellers, who will bring the price up to create liquidity from breakout.

Here is a diagram of a bullish Sponsor candle:

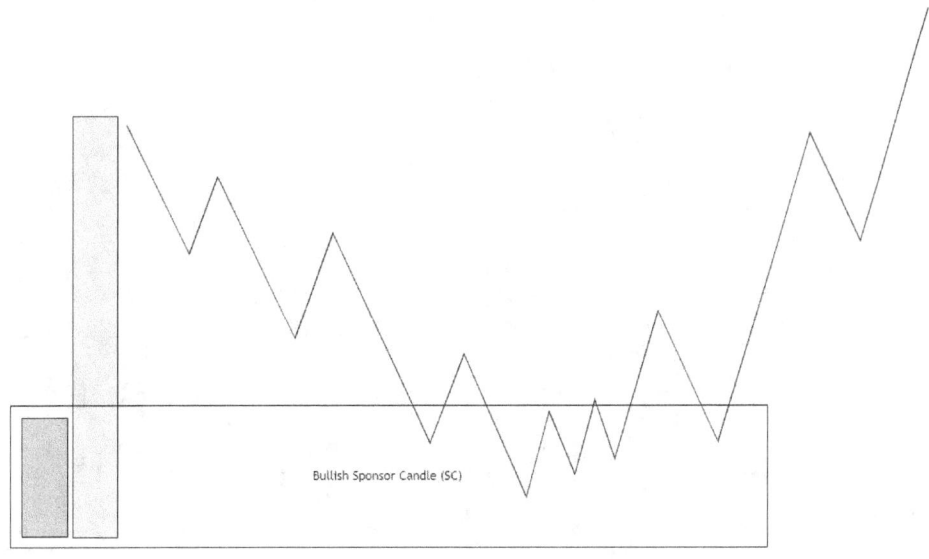

Bullish Sponsor Candle (SC)

Here is a diagram of a bearish Sponsor candle:

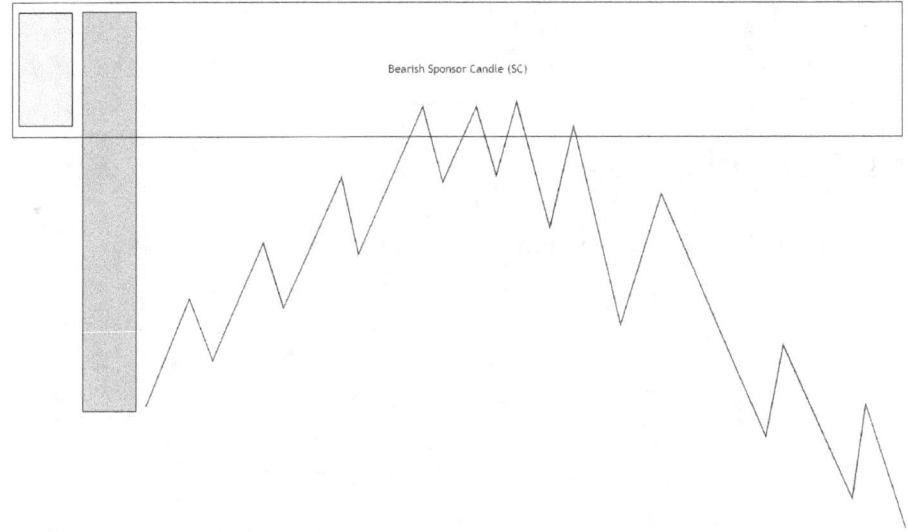

Bearish Sponsor Candle (SC)

Images below show few examples of Sponsor candles:

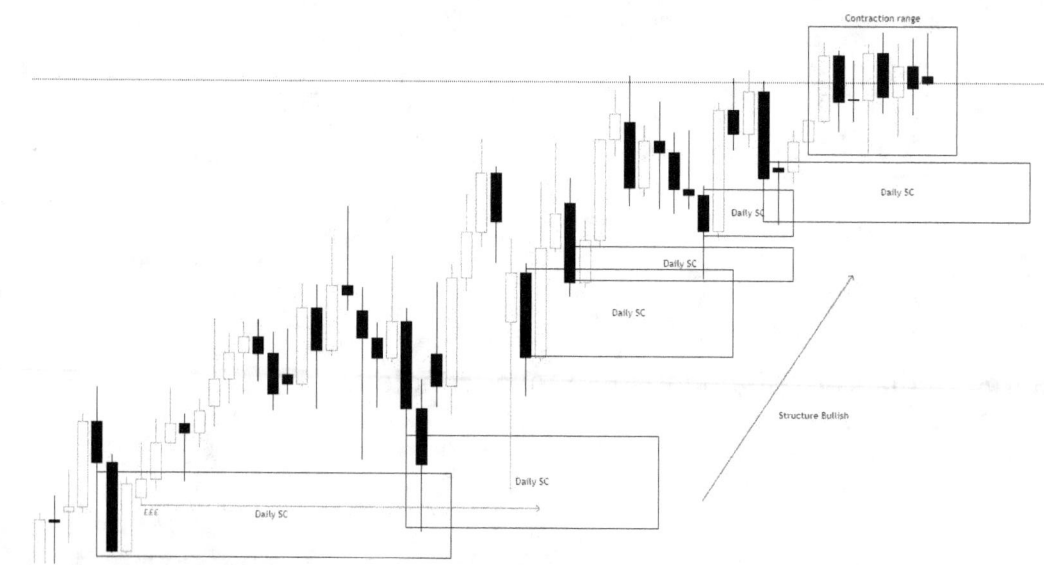

Contraction range

Daily SC

Daily SC

Daily SC

Daily SC

Structure Bullish

Daily SC

Daily SC

EEE

<u>Sponsor Candle Observations</u>

A SC can be valid for a very long time unless it's already been mitigated/depleted. Remember, a SC is created because there wasn't enough liquidity to fill all the orders before a break of structure. Price will want to come back to pick those leftover orders and continue the movement.

Higher time frame sponsor candles tend to be respected more than the ones on the smaller time frame. Also sponsor candles in direction of overall trend on HTF will work out more often.

To determine the strength of SC, ask these questions:

How fast has the price moved away from SC?

When price moved away, has it created strong imbalances?

Has price broken minor or major market structure?

INSTITUTIONAL CANDLE

What Is a Institutional candle

When the banks establish their price structure and or ranges within any currency pair, the future order flow is based on certain levels of the preceding trading range.

Sometimes critical levels can be over shot due to orders being to strong and or cap levels not being maintained. When price dives deep or sells off into a substantial low breaking previous lows with out reacting or bouncing after the liquidity was targeted, this one time creates thin liquidity normally resulting in a sharp counter move back to the original point of origin. However if the market makers display interest in the new re pricing range, they may just mitigate there loss or re structure the loss and wind off those previous longs at the point where the liquidity was tapped into below the previous lows.

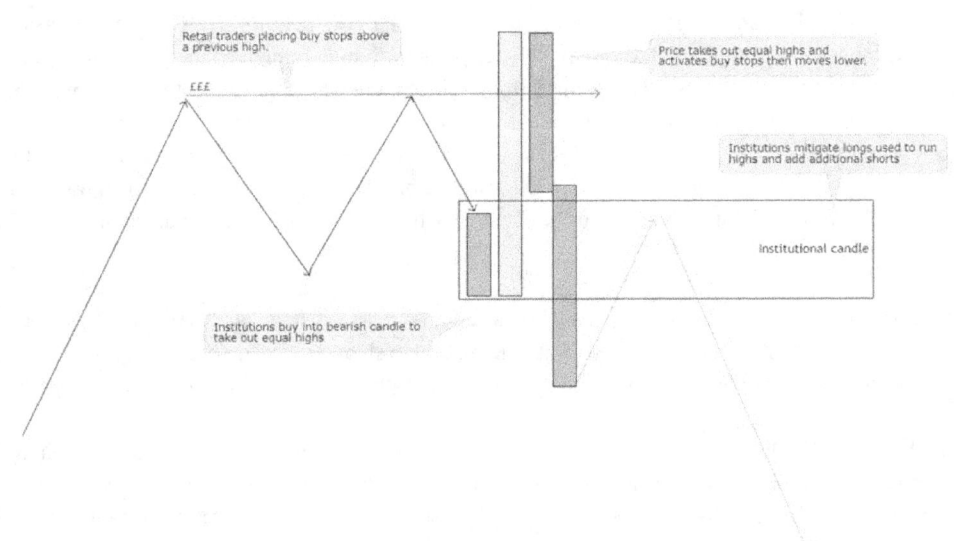

The Backbone

The backbone of getting the perfect entry mirrors very closely to the concept of support and resistance as mentioned previously. A bullish 'Institutional candle' is created by a down move that precedes an up move that resumes the trend, makes new highs and/or breaks market structure. This signifies a move by larger/Institutional sized market participants in which price is driven lower to not only shake out participants, but also to buy the currency at a lower price as well. This zone is then protected by the institutional players the next time the market moves back to that range, as it is their goal to sell at a higher price than they bought at that level. We want to highlight this down move by highlighting that specific candle with a certain colour that identifies Institutions are in the market. We will then place a horizontal ray and note on the line: the timeframe the candle formed, if it Bullish/bearish candle, then illustrate the open of the candle and the middle; the middle of the candle we will caption MTH (stand for 'mean thresh hold'). By putting these horizontal lines allows us to constantly monitor these Institutional candles constantly.

Theses Institutional candles can be drawn on any timeframe, for stronger confluences it is best to go from the highest timeframe down. This will build up a stronger confluence in that section. The higher the timeframe the Institutional candle is formed, the bigger reaction we may witness.

Furthermore, if price reacts of a Institutional candle, but then comes back to that same area a numerous number of times, this illustrates that the Institutional candle is losing strength. This is due to the powers that be who are "protecting" these levels those interests or the capital needed to prevent price from dropping below the Institutional candle. Similar to when support flips resistance, the bullish Institutional candle will then act as resistance when price breaks below it.

Live Example:

SLH

£££

£££

1HR institutional candle (IC)

Entry upon the
mitigation of the
IC

Institutional candle: The last down
candle that was the catalyst to the
impulsive bullish move that swept
previous engineered highs and
created a SLH (Stop loss hunt)

Target: Sweep
of engineered
lows

ENTRY TYPES

We can categorize entries based on various conditions.

First let's look at entries based on SC refinement and existence of LTF confirmation.

Entry 1 - Risk entry

Risky entry is best when your trade is in the direction of the trend and momentum.
You've identified a SC on HTF and refined it on the LTF. So an example would be a 4H SC refined
to the 15m. When all the necessary multiple confluences you require to take a trade are present,
you can set a limit order on refined 15m SC for entry. There is minimal confirmation for entry
therefore the likelihood of being stopped out is increased.

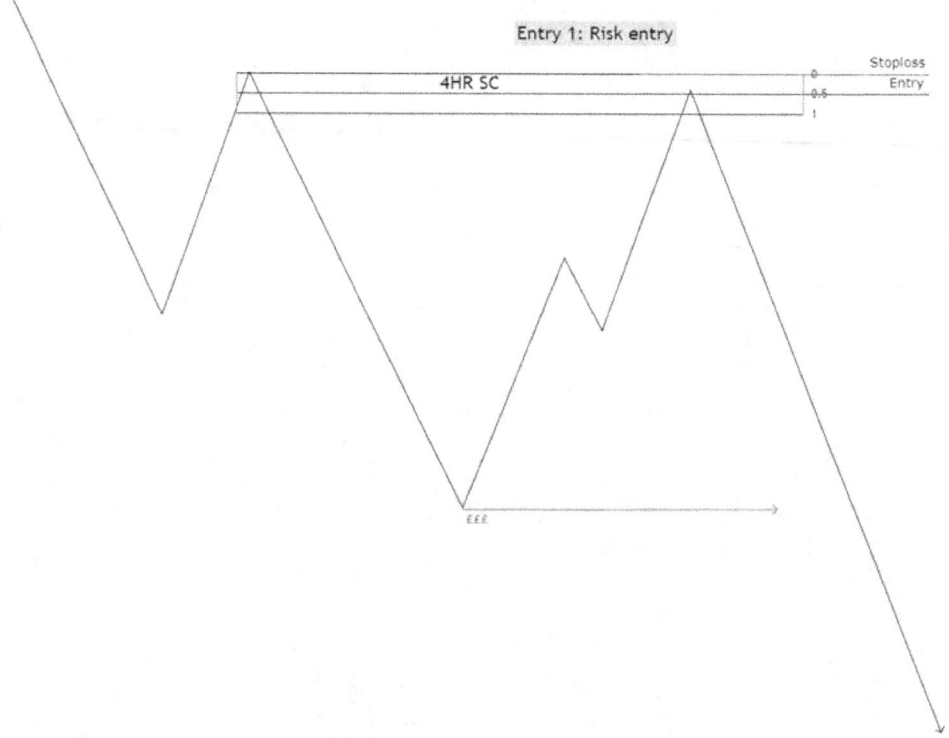

Entry 1: Risk entry

Entry 2 - Justification entry

Justification entry is best when price is moving back to your SC aggressively, you're looking to take a counter trend trade or when there are multiple SCs to consider. Waiting for a BMS to occur on a LTF in the direction of the trend gives you additional confirmation to take that trade more safely than simply setting a limit order. The disadvantage of this entry type is that you may miss some trades because price will come into your area of interest and then it moves away from it very fast without giving you opportunity to enter.

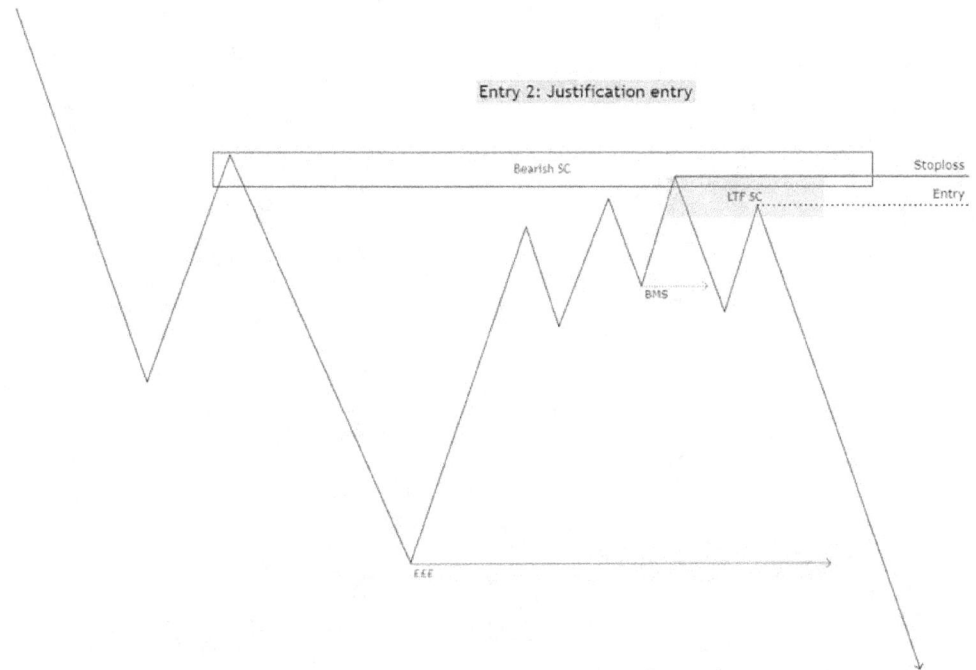

Now let's look at entries based on whether HTF trend has been confirmed or not.

After reversal when we get first BMS (new trend hasn't been confirmed yet), we are looking at Entry 1 - risk entry. After additional BMS when new trend has been confirmed, we are looking at Entry 2 - justification entry. This is illustrated on the images below for bullish and also for bearish scenario.

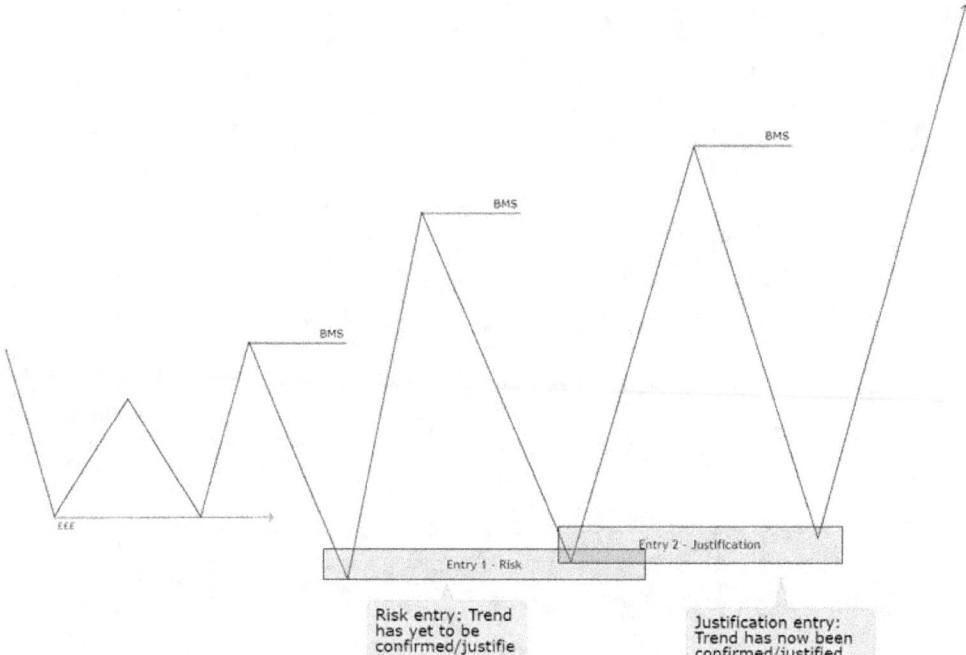

BMS

BMS

BMS

EEE

Entry 1 - Risk

Entry 2 - Justification

Risk entry: Trend
has yet to be
confirmed/justifie
d

Justification entry:
Trend has now been
confirmed/justified

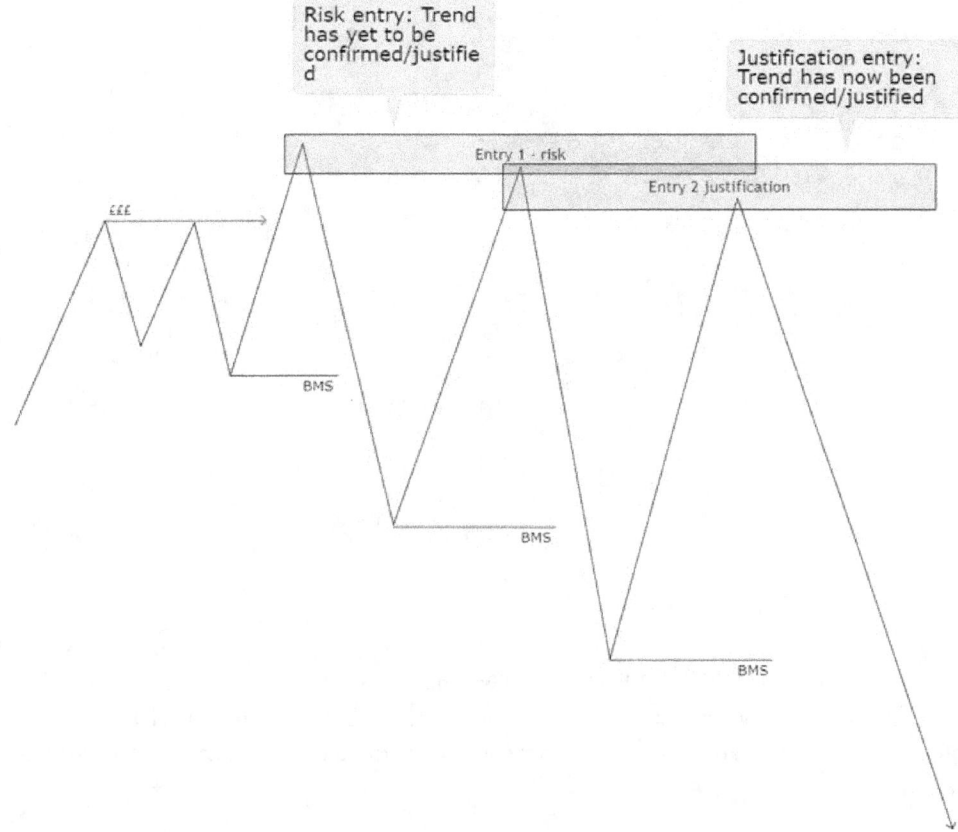

We know that markets are fractal and what you see on higher time frames you will also see on the lower time frames. On the image below you can see, that you can decide how much confirmation you need on multiple time frames to take a trade.

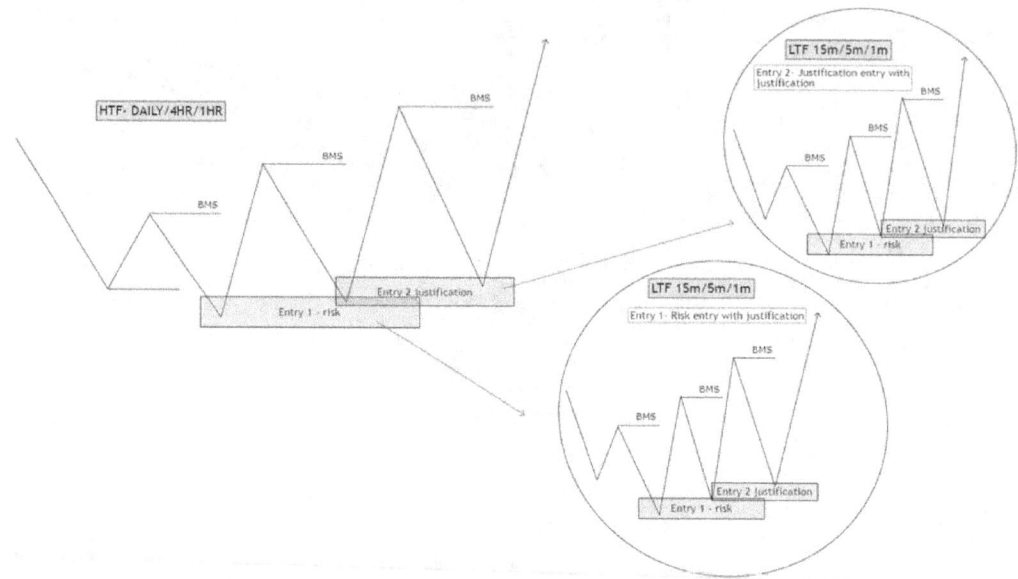

Even after you see BMS on HTF and also LTF has BMS inside your AOI, you could still consider entering trade here risky. What you can do is to wait for trend confirmation on LTF to give you additional confidence to take a trade. In this scenario, you would be using Entry 1 - risk entry with justification.

If using risk entry with justification is still risky for you, you can wait for trend confirmation on HTF. Once we get additional BMS on HTF and trend has been confirmed, you select your AOI. Then you zoom in into LTF and you observe price action as it is approaching your AOI. Here you have two options. First option is riskier and you take a trade once you see BMS. Second option is to wait for confirmation of the trend on the LTF. After additional BMS, when trend is confirmed, you can take the entry. In this scenario, you would be using Entry 2 - Justification entry with justification.

IMBALANCE

What is Imbalance

Imbalance in price is when price moves too fast and it leaves inefficiencies behind. Let's use image below to illustrate how we find the imbalance on the chart. Price was initially moving higher and then we can see five consecutive bearish candles representing strong selling. I have marked first three bearish candles of this move down with numbers 1, 2 and 3. Candle No.2 is usually the largest and it shows that sellers were in charge with not many buyers interested to jump in and stop the price from falling lower. Candle No.2 must close below the candle No.3 high. Now we mark candle No.1 low and candle No.3 high. The distance between these two points is 'Imbalance'.

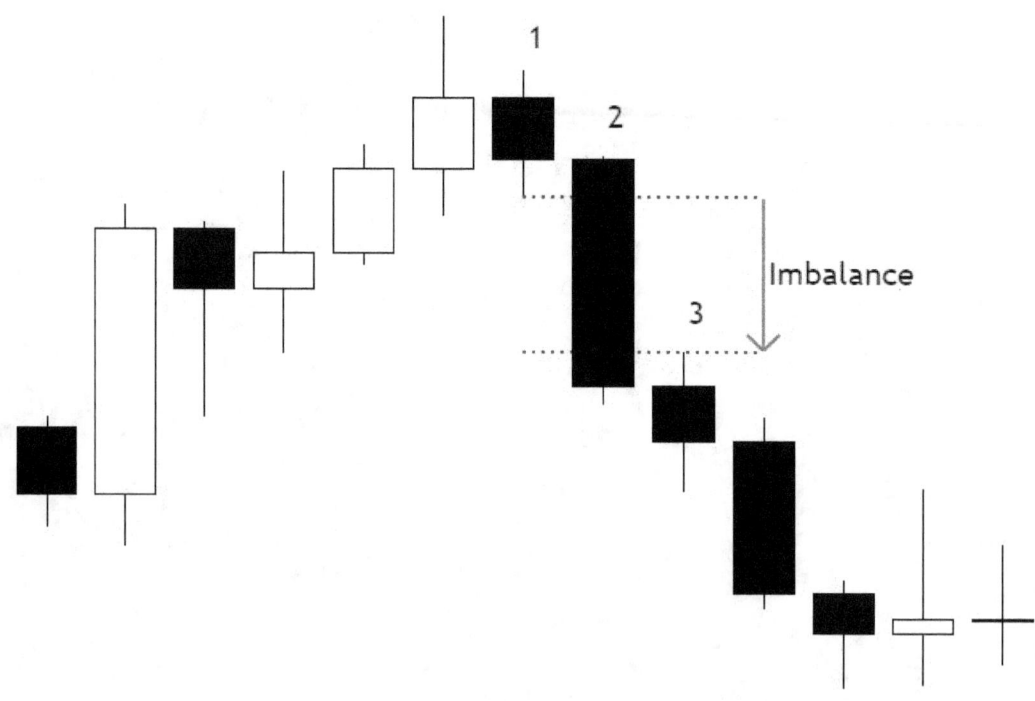

We generally will stick to the higher time frames when looking at imbalance in prices 1 hour and higher. This provides the best range, whereas if you use a lower time frame imbalance, it may only be few pips, which isn't overly helpful. One thing to note is that imbalance is more of an additional confluence and reference point of where price may revisit.

If you spot imbalance on the 1 hour, for example, and you drill down low enough you're likely to see efficient price action overall. That being said you will also see correlating inefficiency in some cases which can be a strong indication of where price is going to revisit if it corelates with a higher timeframe point of imbalance.

Monthly imbalance inline with your AOI on the monthly TF

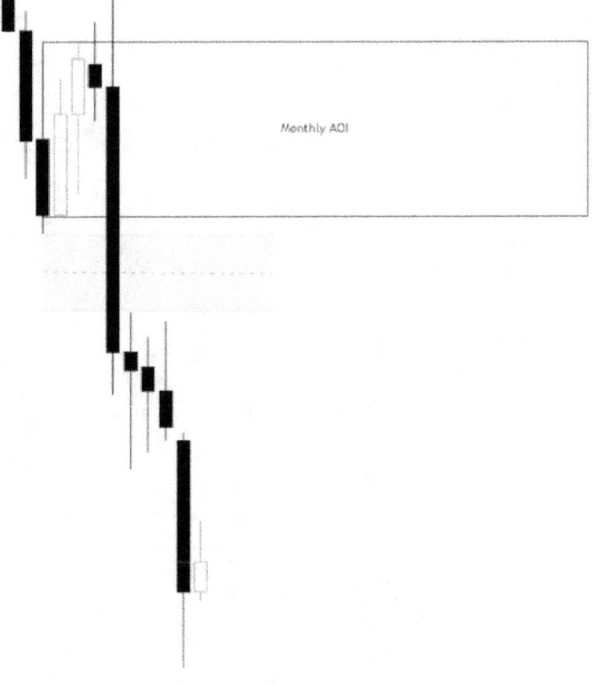

Upon re-balancing with previous imbalance price, we reacted of that monthly AOI that raided previous monthly engineered lows

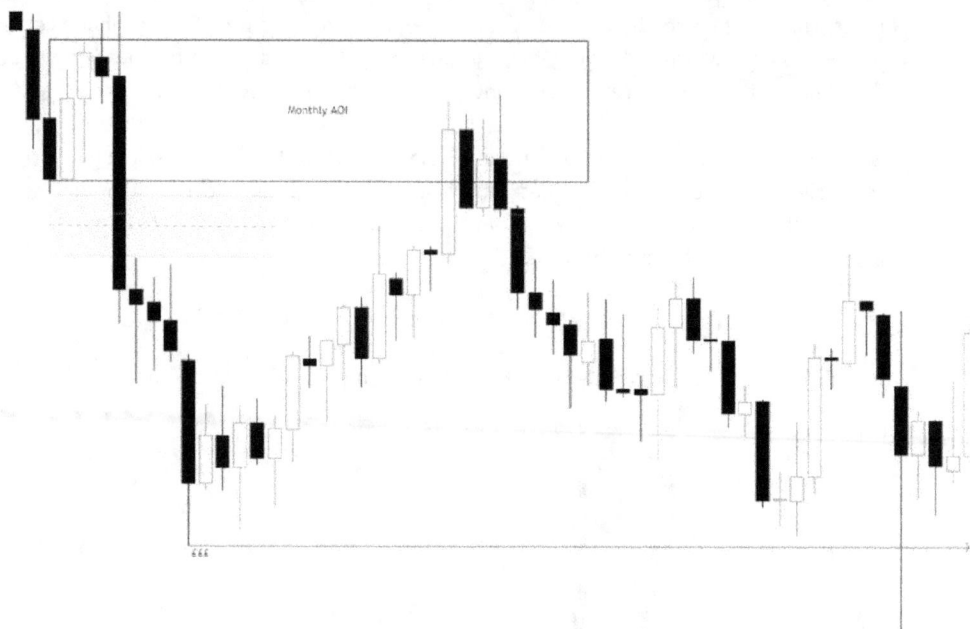

PREMIUM AND DISCOUNT

When we are buying something, we like to look around to find the lowest price or the best discount. When we are trying to sell something, we are looking for someone who is willing to pay the highest price possible, so we can make the most profit. Same applies to the participants in the financial markets.

For example, when you're buying gold, you wait for price to come down to get the best price. When you're selling gold, you wait for price to go higher in order to give you higher profit potential when the price starts to go lower again.

But how do we know when something is cheap enough to buy and expensive enough to sell? There are numerous participants in the financial markets and all of them are looking at the charts in a different way. Some are buyers and some are sellers at the same price. They look at different time frames and have different time or price targets on when to get out of the market.

To find premium and discount levels, we select the impulsive price swing on the time frame we use to analyze the trend. We usually use Fibonacci tool. Once we applied it to the impulsive price swing, 50% level represents the Equilibrium (EQ). Above EQ is Premium range and below EQ is Discount range. We will look for selling opportunities in the premium levels and buying opportunities in the discount levels.

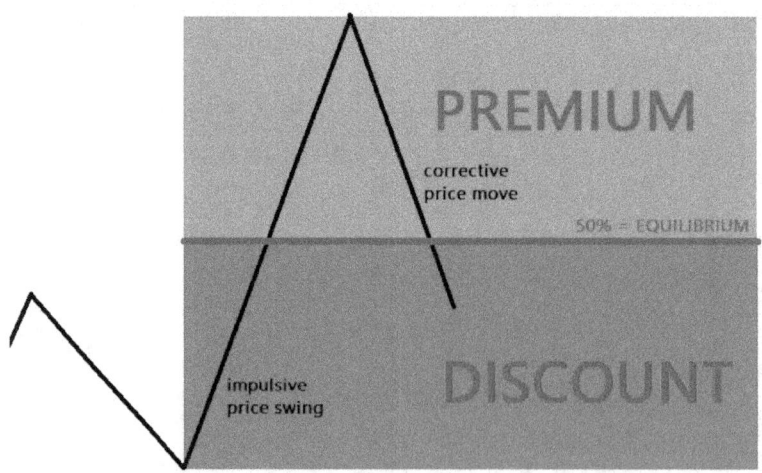

When the market is in a bullish trend and begins to retrace lower, look for a drop below 50% of the Price Run Higher. A drop below 50% (Equilibrium) indicates that price is now in a Discount.

This illustrates that funds and big banks are getting in the best price possible (a discount price range).

Here is an example below:

As we can see from this example, we have a bullish trend present. The bullish trend started when liquidity was taken from the previous low. This liquidity was then used to send GBPUSD in a bullish direction, as price had broken market structure, we understand that price now has reversed. Now we can start looking for entries upon a retracement. In this example we have a retracement into a 'discount price' range and into a Institutional candle so banks are simultaneously buying at a discount price, whilst mitigating with a Institutional candle and adding additional buy positions at that specific point.

As we can see, the current market structure is bearish. After a market makes a run lower and begins to retrace higher, look for a rise above 50% Equilibrium. A rise above 50% or Equilibrium indicates that price is now in a Premium. In this example we have equal highs present with a Sponsor candle above. So we can expect price to liquidate these equal highs and react bearishly off the OB.

As we can see in this example we have successfully raided the equal highs, reacted bearish off the SC and banks took price into a premium pricing in order to get the best value possible on GBPUSD to sell price much lower; as we have witnessed in this example.